Angel Blessings

RECOGNIZING ANGELS IN YOUR LIFE

Ellen Pill Blooming, Ph.D.
Christine Dallman
June Eaton
Marie D. Jones
Carol McAdoo Rehme
Carol Stigger

 Publications International, Ltd.

Contributing Writers:

Ellen Pill Blooming, Ph.D., is contributing editor for *Discovery Girls* magazine. She has collaborated on numerous inspirational books, including *Blessed by an Angel, Echoes of Love: Baby, God's Promise for Teens, Church Chuckles,* and *Toasts for Any Occasion.* Her stories and articles have been published in *Whispers From Heaven* and *Girl's Life* magazines. Dr. Blooming currently has two feature-length screenplays in the works.

Christine Dallman is the author of *Daily Devotions for Seniors* and a contributor to numerous other publications, including *How to Let God Help You Through Hard Times* and *One-Minute Bible Devotions.* She currently resides in Everett, WA.

June Eaton, an extensively published author, has contributed to more than 20 books, and her articles and stories have appeared in more than 50 Christian periodicals. She is also a teacher with a Master of Arts from Northwestern University.

Marie D. Jones is an ordained minister and a contributing author to numerous books, including the *Echoes of Love* series, *A Mother's Daily Prayer Book,* and *When You Lose Someone You Love: A Year of Comfort.* She is also the creator/producer of Gigglebug Farms Simply Storybook Children's Videos.

Carol McAdoo Rehme, a firm believer in the power of stories, publishes prolifically in the inspirational market. Her inspirational and humorous stories appear widely in anthologies, series books, magazines, and national publications. A freelance author, editor, and ghostwriter, she has coauthored seven books. The latest is *Chicken Soup for the Empty Nester's Soul* (2008).

Carol Stigger is an award-winning communications consultant, teacher, and freelance writer specializing in international social justice issues and travel. Her inspirational work appears in several local and national publications, including *Christian Science Monitor, Guideposts, Chicago Tribune, Vital Christianity,* and *Providence Journal.* She is also the author of *Opportunity Knocks.*

Additional Contributing Writers:
Carol Smith, Kelly Womer, Anna Trimiew

Acknowledgments:

All Scripture quotations are taken from *The Holy Bible, New International Version.* Copyright © 1973, 1978, 1984, International Bible Society. Used by permission of Zondervan Publishing House. All rights reserved.

Cover photos: **PhotoDisc.com** (inset); **Stockbyte**

Contents

Recognizing the Angels
  Around You 4

A Brief Encounter 6

A New Dawn 10

Angel at the Intersection . .12

A Helping Hand 14

Promise of an Angel 16

The New Boss 20

Angel in a '57 Chevy 23

Angel in Training 26

A Simple Blessing 28

An Angelic Allowance . . .30

Button's Final Gift 32

Cents and Sensibility 36

A Few Choice Words . . .40

Misty 41

My Lucky Day 43

The Bouquet 45

The Light Within 47

The Little Angel 51

A Close Call 54

Have a Heart 57

Making Mercy
  Out of Leftovers 59

Angels Seen and
  Unseen 63

Pass It On 67

Reading Davin 69

Spring Flowers
  Say It All 73

The School Angel
  Visits Sydney 75

Up a Tree 79

Used 2/27/14 - 10/18

Recognizing the Angels Around You

Are not all angels ministering spirits sent to serve those who will inherit salvation? Hebrews 1:14

Not many of us reflect often on the presence of angels in our lives. Perhaps this is because they can be easily overlooked in the ordinary disguises they tend to wear. Angels may slip in and out of our lives, or they may remain with us for many years. They may appear in the form of a good friend, a spouse, or even a pet. Occasionally, angels intersect our lives at the most unexpected times, sometimes cloaked as a stranger or clearly revealed in all their heavenly power and glory. However, encounters with angels in this form are rare. The angels that most often touch our lives appear less miraculous and powerful, yet they are indispensable to our journey. And whether we recognize them or not, these angels are everywhere, rendering faithful service from our heavenly Father.

Angel Blessings: Recognizing Angels in Your Life is a compilation of stories, quotes, and prayers that shines a light on the many ways God blesses our lives through angels in our day-to-day walk through life. As you read, perhaps you'll recognize your own brushes with angels—both past and present—that have blessed you along your way.

There are stories of varying lengths and from different walks of life. Some are one page long and can be read as a quick inspiration to begin your day or to give you a lift during a coffee break or lunch break. Longer stories are two or three pages and make for good quiet time or bedtime reading. Quotes and prayers relating to angels are interspersed throughout each section to give you food for thought and opportunity to deeply reflect on the significance and meaning of God's ministry of angels.

You don't need to read this book in any particular order, but you will want to read every word. Each story is unique, revealing a beautiful facet of God's unfailing love for us. It is a love he expresses clearly in the blessings he special delivers through his chosen messengers—the ones we call angels.

IN THE MOST UNLIKELY OF PLACES—WAITING IN YOUR SHADOW, PERHAPS—THE MOST IMPROBABLE OF ANGELS WAITS FOR YOU.

A Brief Encounter

Jessie met an angel on a bus. She would've walked that day, but it was just too hot. The lure of the air-conditioned bus was more than she could resist, regardless of her vow to exercise more and reduce global warming by walking to work. By 8:00 A.M., it was already 95 degrees outside.

So she waited at the stop, checking her watch and tapping her foot. She hated not being in control. Control meant that everything was neat and tidy and predictable, just the way she liked it.

The bus pulled up, and she got on. There were two empty seats in the back. Jessie settled in and put her briefcase on the adjoining seat, making it clear that the seat wasn't available. As the bus filled up, people looked at Jessie's empty seat. She looked away, gazing out the window and filling her mind with thoughts of how to organize her day.

"What a beautiful day!" a voice boomed from the front of the bus, shaking Jessie from her organizational reverie. A large, boisterous woman was digging around in her pockets. The bus driver became impatient and motioned for her to go toward the back and sit down. She winked at the people in the front of the bus as she noisily moved toward the back. Jessie shifted her gaze back toward the window and put her hand on her briefcase.

"Excuse me, Miss," said the woman.

Jessie kept her gaze focused on the window and tightened the grip on her bag and her purse.

"Okay if I sit here?"

Jessie reluctantly looked up at the woman's wide grin.

"Um, sure," she replied. Hesitant, Jessie removed her briefcase from the seat and scrunched herself toward the window as far away from the woman as possible.

"What a beautiful day!" cried the woman. Jessie thought this woman didn't seem able to speak below a shout.

Jessie looked out the window and tried to get farther away still.

"Oh, I get it. You think I'm going to give you cooties," the woman said, laughing the most joyous laugh Jessie had ever heard.

It was so much easier to avoid these people when they weren't sitting right next to you, talking directly to you, Jessie thought. Jessie squirmed and remained quiet.

"Come on!" shouted the woman, "Let's talk about it."

"No, thank you," remarked Jessie. "I'm fine, really."

"You're fine?" The boisterous laugh ringing out again. "Now, I'd say that I'm fine. But you? I can see that it's a beautiful day, and I knew that if I got on this bus with a smile the bus driver would let me ride even though I don't have enough money for the fare. And I'm happy as a clam because it's so nice and cool in here. Yep, *I'm* fine. But you?"

"That's very nice," Jessie said quietly, feeling uncomfortable.

"You want me and everyone like me to be quiet. You don't want to see or hear anything that doesn't fit nice and tidy into your life, right?"

"What are you talking about? And why must you shout?"

The woman then started speaking quietly.

"I don't have to shout now, because you're listening to me."

Suddenly, Jessie couldn't *not* listen.

"You look at things, but you don't *see*. You listen to things, but you don't *hear*. You say things that have no *meaning*, and you don't feel things with your *heart*."

Jessie looked away again, feeling like she had the wind knocked out of her. Of all the nerve! How could anyone speak to her like that?

"I don't know who you think—" Now Jessie was the one shouting. But Jessie was shouting at no one. The seat beside her was empty, and her briefcase was on the seat. The bus had stopped, and the woman was getting off. No one else entered or exited. It wasn't even a bus stop. The woman smiled at Jessie one last time. She smiled that big, full-toothed, without-a-care-in-the-world smile. For a moment, Jessie felt warmed down to the depth of her soul.

But why should she be happy? That woman was so rude! As the bus pulled away from the curb, Jessie looked out the window for the woman. She looked up and down the street, but the woman had vanished.

"Must've gone into her house or something," Jessie told herself, trying to make sense of it. The man across the aisle from Jessie raised his eyebrows at her as she looked around the bus to see if anyone else had noticed the woman disappear.

"What a strange woman, huh?" Jessie didn't normally speak to strangers at all, even a well-dressed man like this one, but she desperately needed someone to acknowledge this woman's presence.

The man looked at her, tilting his head sideways, not unlike the way Jessie had looked at the woman. "What woman?" was all he said before he turned, pretending to be interested in something outside.

All day at work, the woman was the only thing on Jessie's mind. That day, she smiled more than usual. She went out at lunch and noticed how the sunlight warmed her bare arms. The man behind the lunch counter where she ate every day had a nice smile. For the first time, Jessie thought maybe she really *was* fine. In fact, she was better than she'd been in a long time.

EVERY TIME WE MAKE A FRIEND, AN ANGEL SMILES IN HEAVEN.

A New Dawn

S arah had a loving husband, a beautiful daughter, an affectionate dog, and a great job. She and her husband were friends with several couples they enjoyed. They all had children the same age and went to the same church. They even hired babysitters and went to the symphony, a baseball game, or just out to dinner sometimes.

Sarah was happy—but she wasn't content. She went to church every Sunday, but one day it dawned on her that she didn't really know how to pray. It was as if all this goodness in her life didn't matter if she couldn't share it with God.

Then early one Saturday morning, their dog, Betsy, woke up Sarah. This was very unusual, so she knew that Betsy must really need to go out. They went out to the backyard together in the warm summer morning. Sarah grew increasingly annoyed when all Betsy did was sit next to her. She pondered how much more sleep she'd be able to get before the kids woke her up. Suddenly, Betsy barked and ran around to the side of the house. Sarah followed and looked to the horizon above the empty lot across the street. She was stunned by what she saw—an exquisite dawn. The colors were unbelievably beautiful.

Sarah was surprised to find tears rolling down her cheeks as she witnessed the miracle of this dawn. "Thank you, Betsy. Good girl." She was kneeling beside her dog now, holding her close. The emptiness in Sarah's heart began to fill.

Ever so slowly, without realizing what she was doing, Sarah began to pray. Then she thanked God for Betsy. Who knew God's messenger could be a dog?

Lord in Heaven,

Please help me to see the angels

that I know you have placed in my presence.

Help me to slow down and know that I am always

divinely protected and guided.

And guide me toward your angels

to spread your word, do your work,

be kind, and love.

Thank you, Lord, for your help this day.

EACH MORNING AT DAWN, THE ANGELS AWAKEN AND PAINT THE SKY WITH MIRACLES.

*A*ngel at the *I*ntersection

*A*fter two weeks of walking my kindergartener, Alec, to and from school every day, we had gotten to know the different crossing guards from the busy intersection near our house by name. I explained that crossing guards help children cross streets safely and that he should always mind them.

Alec loved kindergarten, especially the playground. Sometimes we would walk there after supper. He would show me how high he could swing and how far he could climb on the monkey bars.

One Saturday, he came in from playing with a scraped knee. After wiping his tears and applying a cartoon-character bandage, I found out that he had fallen off one of the playground swings. Although he knew he was not supposed to cross the street alone to go to the playground, he did not act like he had misbehaved. I didn't get far with my lecture because he assured me that the crossing guard had helped him across the street both ways. I could not believe he was lying to me, so we walked to the school together. But no crossing guard was in sight. I asked him which guard had helped him, and he said he had never seen her before.

The next school day, Alec and I went together to talk to the principal about the crossing guard. He told us that guards never worked on Saturdays. When Alec described the woman, the principal turned pale. "That sounds like Mrs. Anna," he said. "Are you sure that she had short gray hair and glasses?"

Alec nodded solemnly.

The principal told Alec to go to his classroom, then turned to me and said, "I can't explain it. Mrs. Anna was a crossing guard for ten years, but she died over the summer."

EACH OF US HAS OUR OWN ANGELS TO GUIDE AND DIRECT US. A BELOVED FRIEND, A TRUSTED MENTOR, OR A FAMILY MEMBER WE CAN ALWAYS DEPEND ON. ANGELS ARE EVERYWHERE.

Heavenly Father, our hearts are full of gratitude for the encouragement, comfort, and support you provide for us through your angels. Our faith is strengthened as we feel their supportive presence. Our lives are changed through their daily vigil and intervention as they protect us from wrong decisions, guide us through difficult situations, and provide us with joyful surprises. In response, may we always be ready to reach out to others in your name.

ANGELS TAKE DELIGHT IN THE MIRACLE OF EACH NEW DAY.

A Helping Hand

Lourdes already hated getting a cab in the city, but being eight months pregnant made matters even worse. Add the fact that it was pouring rain, and it was the making of a lousy morning.

She had always thought that pregnant women would have no trouble getting cabs, but it seemed manners were in short supply as cab after cab was taken by some inconsiderate person in a suit and tie trying to get to work on time. Lourdes was about to give up, but she had no car and had to get to her doctor's for a prenatal appointment.

The pains began slowly, and Lourdes almost laughed out loud at the perfect irony. Murphy's Law, she thought. Whatever could go wrong would go wrong, and now she was going into labor on the sidewalk in New York City.

Out of the blue, a man in a black suit stepped off the curb and waved down a cab. Lourdes watched as the cab stopped immediately. She was about to scream that it should have been her cab when the man turned to her and waved his arm, indicating that she should take the ride. Relieved, Lourdes accepted, walking past the man, who simply winked at her. The man leaned over and told the driver to take her to the hospital immediately. Wondering how he knew her destination, Lourdes turned to confront her Good Samaritan, but he was nowhere in sight.

"What a nice man," the cab driver remarked. Lourdes simply nodded her head in agreement. Sometimes an angel can wear a suit and tie.

———— ⋇ ————

DON'T LOOK FOR HALOS OR WINGS OR LONG WHITE ROBES. THE ANGELS IN YOUR LIFE ARE MORE LIKELY TO BE WEARING BLUE JEANS AND SNEAKERS. JUST LOOK FOR THE LIGHT IN THEIR EYES AND THE WARMTH OF THEIR SMILES.

———— ⋇ ————

Never let our need overshadow our recognition of the needs of others. Ground us in empathy. Commission our sympathy. Urge us to offer comforting hands and understanding hearts. And in so doing, show us how easing the pain of others eases our own.

———— ⋇ ————

MOST ANGELS WE ENCOUNTER IN THIS LIFE WEAR DISGUISES. IT'S NOT SURPRISING, THEN, THAT WE ARE RARELY ABLE TO DETECT THEM EXCEPT IN THANKFUL RETROSPECT.

Promise of an Angel

Nothing makes a doctor happier than to tell his patients that they are well again. For Gina, hearing those words from her own doctor made her feel like she had a new lease on life. She had dealt with the harsh realities of breast cancer and the exhausting regimen of treatment for two years, and now she appeared to be in remission.

Gina knew she could never have done it without the loving care of the nurses at Regents Hospital, and she had promised them she would come back often and help them with their new volunteer program reading to cancer patients. But, of course, when the nurses did call, Gina was swamped with catching up on her job and had to decline several times. Each time she felt as though she was not only letting them down, but letting herself down, too. But she was concerned with her workload and figured she would get around to the reading program as soon as things calmed down.

One afternoon, after a hectic day of meetings, Gina collapsed in the break room, dizzy and weak, and she was immediately taken to the hospital. Terrified that her cancer had made a surprise comeback, she nervously waited for her doctor to come with the news. But this time the news was good; she had only been dehydrated. Her doctor reprimanded her for not taking better care of herself and told her to slow down. Gina promised she would do a better job.

As she left the hospital, Gina ran into one of the nurses who had set up the volunteer program. The nurse smiled and asked Gina if she would be able to come in the next day to read to a special new patient. Gina was about to object and ask if she could do it some other time when another nurse wheeled a young child toward them. The little girl was bald and looked pale and weak, but she managed a faint smile.

"This is Abby," the nurse said to Gina. Gina smiled and gently took the girl's hand. "She is new here, but we already love her like crazy," the nurse said, winking at Abby, who winked back.

"Will you be the one reading to me tomorrow?" Abby asked softly, looking up at Gina with dark eyes that seemed to hide how tired she truly was. Gina fought back tears as she whispered "yes."

The next day, Gina rearranged several meetings and headed to the hospital to read to Abby. Once in Abby's room, Gina found the girl eagerly anticipating the story of her choice, which was a Nancy Drew mystery. Gina had loved Nancy Drew as a child, and she felt an immediate bond with this lovely girl, who she later discovered was terminally ill.

Gina read to Abby, but most of the time they just talked about other things, such as Abby's family, her favorite movies, and her friends. Abby was a smart girl with a curiosity Gina found endearing. They had so much in common and became fast friends in just that quick hour.

For three weeks, Gina went to the hospital every other day to read to Abby, going through at least five Nancy Drew

books. One day, Gina brought Abby a signed copy of an original Nancy Drew novel she had won on eBay. It had cost her a lot of money, but the look on Abby's face was priceless. Abby's mom was there, too, and she gave Gina a warm hug in the hallway, saying, "Thank you for caring so much about our little girl." It made Gina feel good to help someone, especially when she had been helped so much when she was going through cancer herself.

The following week, Gina was unable to visit Abby for a few days, having caught the flu that was going around the office. When she was finally feeling better and had received the green light to go back to the hospital, she went to see her favorite patient. She practically ran down the hallway, so excited to see her pal. But when she reached Abby's room, she was greeted with an empty bed. She looked for the first nurse she could find, and Gina learned that Abby had passed away the day before. Her heart broke, and she had to sit down to prevent her from losing her balance.

"Are you Gina?" the nurse asked. Gina nodded, wiping away her tears.

"Abby left something for you," said the nurse. "Hold on a second and let me get it for you." The nurse walked quickly over to the nurse's station and returned with a small envelope. She handed the envelope to Gina and left her alone to read it.

On the outside of the envelope, Abby had written Gina's name, dotting the "i" with a tiny pink heart. Inside was a note, also written in pink marker:

Dear Gina,

Thank you for reading to me and for being my angel. I will never forget you.

Love, Abby

Gina cried fresh tears and held the note against her heart. She whispered to herself, "I'll never forget you either, Abby." Even as waves of sorrow passed through her, she felt a sense of joy knowing that she had kept her promise to the nurses and that she had been an angel to someone who needed her.

NO DREAM IS UNREACHABLE WHEN YOU HAVE ANGELS BY YOUR SIDE. THEIR WINGS BECOME YOURS, AND TOGETHER YOU SOAR.

Father in heaven, let me be an angel to someone today. Just as you have blessed my life with people who love and cherish me, let me be a light of love that shines upon someone who needs me. I have received the gift of angels, now allow me to give and be one in return.

The New Boss

The only thing worse than getting used to a new job is having to find your footing around a boss you know nothing about. Nancy wasn't looking forward to getting to know Mr. Jenkins, the man her new fellow employees called "The Master." Even though she was thrilled to be working at the advertising agency with the best reputation in town, she dreaded her first meeting with her new boss and wondered if she should ask around for advice. She was coming in as a vice president, having made a name for herself at a rival agency, but she felt like she was starting from scratch.

The only information Nancy could get out of her colleagues was to be prepared for the worst. She felt sick to her stomach going into Mr. Jenkins' spacious office that afternoon, and she felt faint as she waited for him to enter.

She was a bit shocked when a very small, stocky man came into the room and firmly shook her hand. He introduced himself and asked Nancy her name, even though she knew that he had her file on his desk in front of him.

They talked for a brief ten minutes. Mr. Jenkins did all the talking, while Nancy listened and nodded attentively at just the right moments. He explained to her what he expected from her, which was nothing short of miracles for his beloved company. When the meeting ended, Nancy ran to the lunchroom and made herself a hot cup of tea to calm her nerves.

For the next year, Nancy worked hard to satisfy the demanding Mr. Jenkins. Sometimes she did well, other times he sent her back to completely redo something with a firm critique that always, although not personal, made her feel tiny and worthless. Mr. Jenkins was a force to be reckoned with, but Nancy liked her work, and she needed her job. She was supporting her elderly mother and had a mortgage and medical bills to pay.

A few months later, it was Nancy who became ill. She ended up in the hospital with pneumonia and was confined to bed rest. Her hospital stay extended to weeks, and she tried to call her office and take on any work possible, but she could do very little. She accepted the fact that she would probably lose her job and wondered if she had brought the disease upon herself with the stress and heavy workload she had undertaken.

On the first day of her fourth week in the hospital, Nancy actually began feeling better. She decided to bite the bullet and call Mr. Jenkins directly, if only to find out who had replaced her. As she dialed his number on the phone by her bed, the door to her room opened, and the man himself came in, holding a huge vase of flowers and a teddy bear.

Mr. Jenkins sat beside Nancy's bed for three hours, talking and laughing with her and assuring her that she would have her job waiting for her when she left the hospital. He even shared a softer side of himself, telling her how he had started the company with nothing and worked through the loss of his wife and the death of his first business partner. As she sat there listening, Nancy felt that this man whom everyone feared was really a sweet, hard-working man with a vision. She realized that she greatly admired him.

Before he left, Mr. Jenkins put his hand on Nancy's shoulder and said, "Don't worry. You will be taken care of. We'll see you back at the office soon."

He left, and Nancy fought back a tear, wondering how she could have ever feared such a kind, generous man. Yes, he was firm and demanding, but he was fair. That was all you could ask for in a boss.

Soon, Nancy was on her first day back to work. She was shocked to see the sad expressions of her colleagues as they saw that she was back. But she soon found out why they were upset—the night before, Mr. Jenkins had passed away from a heart attack.

Later that day, Nancy sat with her colleagues, curious about the fate of the company, when they received a phone call from the company's attorneys. Nancy called a meeting of all the employees. She read a letter sent over by the attorneys' office, explaining that the company would continue under the rules of the Jenkins estate, but this time, even to Nancy's surprise, with a new boss at the helm: Nancy.

As her colleagues warmly welcomed their new boss, Nancy smiled to herself and quietly prayed for the angel who had believed in her. At that moment, Nancy promised herself that she would be as fair and kind a boss as Mr. Jenkins had been.

Angel in a '57 Chevy

After I got my driver's license, my father made sure I knew how to change a tire by myself before he let me drive alone. It was pure luck that allowed me to remember how to change the tire when my father tested me on it, and I haven't been able to correctly change a tire since.

Years later, when my first child was an infant, I had a flat tire. It was foggy and raining outside, and I was frightened. Soon, a car pulled up behind me, and a young man got out. "Y'all need help," he said and then proceeded to change the tire. The sentence came out of his mouth like a statement, not a question. We were in New York, and clearly not south of the Mason-Dixon Line. He refused money by rephrasing his greeting, "Y'all needed help." That night, my husband asked what kind of car the man drove, but I had been too distracted to notice.

When I had my next flat tire, I was on my way to visit my parents. My three children were approaching their second hour of bickering, and I had lost my temper miles ago. Although I pulled as far onto the shoulder as possible, half the car was still on the narrow country road. I hustled the kids out of the car and took off my white sweater to wave and get someone's attention when a car drove by. The car seemed to come out of nowhere. The driver looked vaguely familiar, but it was his voice that I remembered most. "Y'all need help," he said.

Immediately, he set to work, but I grew even more frustrated when my kids' complaining increased another decibel. "Y'all settle down," the man said. Surprisingly, the children obeyed. When he finished changing my flat tire, he followed us in his car to the highway, where his headlights became indistinguishable in the traffic. I remembered the car—a '57 Chevy is a rare sight on the highways these days. Too bad his antique car was so rusty and battered.

At dinner, my mother was sympathetic about my ordeal and gladly offered me a piece of pie. I was relieved that my father was out of town and would not know until tomorrow that I did not know how to change a tire. After the children were asleep, I told my mother that a young man with a Southern accent had changed my tire six years earlier, and I thought it was the same guy.

But my mom was more interested in the '57 Chevy. "Isn't that the car all the kids just had to have?" she asked. She found an old photo album and flipped through the pages. "Remember your cousin Bobby from Louisiana?" she asked.

The summer when I was ten years old, we had visited distant cousins on our way to Florida. She showed me the photo, and I remembered Bobby. He was a teenager at the time, and my father wouldn't let my siblings and me ride in his new car, even though Bobby had promised us ice cream. We had complained about it to our father all the way to Tallahassee. In the black-and-white photo, Bobby was grinning beside a polished '57 Chevy. Looking at the photo, I could almost smell the new leather.

"Bobby died," I said. "He was young, right?"

"He crashed two cars before he and his '57 Chevy slid into Lake Pontchartrain," she replied. "He was only 18."

The next day, my father taught me how to change a tire. He told me that he believed in angels, but considering the way Bobby drove, sooner or later, God might revoke his license.

ANGELS BLEND IN WITH THE CROWD, STAMPING OUT BAD TEMPERS AND PROTECTING TENDER LITTLE TOES.

Lord, I know that you simply cannot be everywhere at once, so you made angels to help you spread your loving grace upon the earth. Thank you for blessing my life with an abundance of angels in the form of friends and family members who love and care for me. They fill my life with joy and give me wings to follow my dreams.

WHEN YOU MOST NEED THEM, GOD SUMMONS HIS ANGELS TO PROTECT YOU FROM DANGER AND LIGHT YOUR WAY HOME.

Angel in Training

My kitchen table was covered with spreadsheets and inventory lists. My friend Megan sat across the table, sympathetically listening to my litany of problems. I could not afford to open my own bookstore, and I did not know how to run a business. My dream had drowned that morning in a sea of red ink, and I was in tears. So many of my dreams had died—I had not finished college, I had one child (not three, like I wanted), and I was divorced.

Megan poured coffee and said, "Are you sure you want to quit now?"

I waited until the noise of our children playing in the other room died before I answered.

"Yes," I started to mutter quietly. But before I could admit my defeat, Anna, Megan's four-year-old, skipped across the kitchen chanting, "Don't walk out on your dreams!"

"Where did she hear that?" I asked.

Megan shrugged. "That's an old song, I think, but I haven't heard it in years. I certainly don't listen to it or ever sing it."

Anna disappeared around a corner, and the noise rose to its former level.

"I think I'm going to run these numbers again," I said, "and get some professional advice."

That was five years ago. I tell my customers that the "A" in my A-to-Z Bookstore stands for Anna, a little angel who stopped playing long enough to deliver a short, sweet, and motivating message.

I am so thankful

for the angels of light

who guide my journey,

and for the angels of wisdom

who whisper to me

what I need to know.

I am so thankful

for the angels of joy

who remind me of the

happiness in my world.

And I am so thankful

for the guardian angel

who is always with me,

keeping me safe.

A Simple Blessing

*I*n her 60-plus years, my mother had never been a patient in the hospital except to deliver her three children. Never, that is, until eight months ago.

It started when she had to have her gallbladder removed, followed by detection of breast cancer, which was followed by a biopsy and surgery for removal of the tumor. That was followed by chemotherapy, radiation, and more chemotherapy. During the first round of chemo, a routine surgery caused a blood clot to form in her neck. As a result, she had to go through yet another surgery.

Recently, when she had a two-week break between chemo and radiation treatments, she and my dad were heading home after a taxing trip to the grocery store. As they were pulling out of the parking lot, there was a tap at my dad's window. A stranger stood outside, holding up a purse.

"Is this yours?" he asked breathlessly, as Dad rolled down his window.

"Oh, my goodness! Yes!" Mom exclaimed. "How did you know to bring it here to us?"

"You were one of two cars leaving the parking lot. I just picked your car," he said, panting as the rain dripped down his face. "I found it in a shopping cart."

I don't know what might have happened to my mom's fragile health if she'd had to cope with losing the contents of her purse. But I do know that the anonymous man who dashed into the rain to return a woman's purse in a simple good deed, was transformed into a real, live angel at that moment.

ANGELS INHABIT A SPECIAL DIMENSION. NOT BOUND BY THE LAWS OF NATURE, THEY ACCOMPLISH THINGS WE CAN ONLY DREAM OF.

Thank you, God, for the salesclerk who took an extra moment to be gracious, for the person who delivered my mail, and for the drivers who yielded to me without hesitation. I do not know their names, but they blessed me today with their hard work and positive attitudes.

OF ALL THE PRESENTS WE MIGHT RECEIVE, THE BEST IS AN ANGEL'S PRESENCE.

An Angelic Allowance

I stood in disbelief as I stared at the crumpled wad of cash on the floor of the convenience store. I had been in this store on numerous occasions, and there had always been a handful of people in there paying for gasoline, picking up snacks or groceries, or using the restrooms. As I stood there, I thought about how it was the middle of the day on a weekend and there should have been lots of customers around, or at least a clerk at the counter. It was like that when I had walked in, but now, just a few moments later, there was no one.

I warily looked around the little mini-mart again, because I was beginning to feel as though I was on one of those television shows with hidden cameras. Finally, I hesitatingly bent over to pick up the folded bills. I gazed out the glass doors to see if someone was checking their pockets or returning to retrieve what they had lost. I saw no one. I felt a small pang of guilt as I put the money in my pocket and waited for the clerk to return from the restroom.

"I found some money on the floor," I told her as I paid for my bottle of water. "I'd like to give you my phone number in case someone calls or comes back looking for it." She took my number, and I left the store, still scanning the parking lot for a possible owner of the cash I'd just inherited.

I returned to my two friends who had been waiting for me. We were on the last day of a three-day bike trip and had stopped to have lunch at a nearby picnic site. I pulled out the bills and counted, "Twenty, forty, sixty, eighty. I just found $80, you guys!" I told them what had happened, and they shared in my joy. "I really need this right now," I said, still aware that someone might claim it but thinking that it was more likely that an angel of mercy had just delivered it to me.

The truth is that I had come on the trip even though I couldn't really afford it. I rationalized by telling myself that I hadn't taken a vacation in a couple of years, and I really felt like I deserved a reprieve from my nonstop schedule. It was October, and another chance to enjoy the outdoors wouldn't happen again until May or June. When all was said and done, I was about $80 over my budget. I'll work some overtime when I get back, I had thought wearily as I packed my backpack before the trip.

After three glorious days surrounded by Mother Nature, I felt positive and refreshed. I was not surprised that no one called to claim the money I'd stumbled upon at the convenience store that day. I did pray for the person who lost it and that God would repay him or her. I like to imagine an unseen angel that day, standing next to those folded bills, as I hesitantly picked up the means for a much-needed rest.

⸻ ➤•◄ ⸻

LISTEN FOR THE WHISPER OF AN ANGEL. IT'S THAT PROMPTING YOU FEEL IN YOUR HEART.

Button's Final Gift

It was a day in early spring where I lived. It would rain and thunder and lightning, then the sun would come out. Then it would rain again. We always said, "Don't like the weather? No matter—it will change in ten minutes!" This particular day, I wanted to get some things cleaned up in the backyard. Our eldest daughter was graduating high school, and I was getting the yard ready for an informal graduation party. I wanted to start pulling some weeds and old plants out of the garden area around the base of our big old oak tree.

The sun came out, and it looked like there might be a break in the weather, so I quickly headed outside and grabbed my gardening gear from the shed. Button, my little terrier, followed me, as usual. She didn't seem too interested in the squirrels today, who were jumping around in our tree teasing her.

I became so lost in my work that I didn't realize it had suddenly grown dark and cloudy again. A few claps of thunder got my attention, but I was so close to unearthing a huge, stubborn weed that I didn't pay any attention.

Button grew tired of sniffing and was lying right beside me, fast asleep. She was an old dog and had been my constant companion for nearly all of her 13 years. I loved her with all my heart. I took her in when she had nowhere to go, and she had taken care of me over the years. It had been a mutual-admiration society.

Button woke up, looked up at me, and barked. That meant that I was supposed to bend down for a kiss. She gave me a sweet little smooch and wandered around to the other side of the tree. There was a special little place back there where I'd ignored her digging, since no one could see it from the house, anyway. It was her favorite spot to lie down in the dirt. I couldn't see her, but I assumed that she'd gone to have another nap.

Another clap of thunder got my attention, and I started working a little faster. The lightning seemed awfully close, and I knew that we needed to get away from the tree. I gathered my things, wondering how Button was sleeping through all of this. I ran to the shed with my gardening tools and headed for the backdoor, expecting Button to appear beside me. I couldn't believe that she was still asleep—she always seemed to have a sixth sense that told her when I was coming or going. I headed back to the tree to look for her, calling her name with increasing concern.

The lightning and thunder were growing worse, and it had started pouring rain. It seemed like the storm was right on top of us. "Button!" I screamed. Then I heard her barking over by the backdoor. Her barking became more intense, and she seemed terrified and wanted to get into the house. I ran to the backdoor to let her in, and just as I moved away from the tree, there was a huge clap of thunder and lightning. Button kept me focused on her as I opened the backdoor, and we ran in. As we went in, I heard a huge crash. Before I could turn around to look outside, Button ran off. I assumed she'd headed upstairs to hide under the bed and wait out the storm.

I looked out into the yard and realized that lightning had struck our beautiful old tree. One huge branch and numerous smaller ones had fallen, right in the spot where I had been standing just seconds before.

It seemed that Button had saved my life with her pleas to come inside. I ran upstairs to find her and thank her. She was nowhere to be found. I checked every hiding place I could think of, but no Button.

Just then my husband, Jim, came home from work. Usually when he walked in the front door, Button bounded out to greet him. Nothing. Where could she have gone?

We searched the house, and finally Jim insisted that she must have gotten out. I tried to explain to him that I had seen her run into the house and that all the doors were closed. I told him that her insistent bark had actually saved me from being outside near the tree when the lightning struck. Still, we couldn't think of anywhere else to look. The sun was shining once again, so we ventured back outside. I looked around the side of the house, and Jim headed for the tree. Seconds later, he was back at my side. I could tell by the look on his face that something was terribly wrong.

"I found her in her spot—" he began. "I don't know what you saw, sweetheart, but Button is lying peacefully in her spot under the tree." There were tears in his eyes as he said, "She was a good old girl."

"But I saw her," I interrupted. Then it hit me. My Button had died under her tree. And so she must've died *before* she saved me from the falling branches. Even as an angel, Button was still looking out for me.

———————— ⟫•⟪ ————————

THERE MUST BE ANGELS, OR ELSE HOW COULD WE FIND PEACE IN THE MIDST OF CHAOS, THANKFULNESS IN THE MIDST OF NEED, HOPE IN THE MIDST OF SORROW? THERE MUST BE ANGELS.

———————— ⟫•⟪ ————————

Lord, you send your angels to us each day when we most need them and least expect them. We thank you for the protection, reassurance, and blessings they offer in your name. Please continue to shower us with these daily reminders of your great love for us and keep us safely tucked beneath the shadow of your angels' wings.

———————— ⟫•⟪ ————————

WHEN YOU LOVE ANOTHER WITH ALL YOUR HEART, YOUR LOVE JOINS WITH THEIRS AND AN ANGEL IS BORN.

Cents and Sensibility

*A*nd to think, you actually volunteered for this, Kate thought to herself, rolling her eyes toward heaven. There better be bountiful blessings for a sacrifice of this magnitude!

With a little vigor, she rang the bell over the Salvation Army's hefty red kettle and tried—without success—to catch the eye of another passing shopper.

All around her, the sights and sounds of Christmas jingled, pressing reminders that the hours were slipping away. People streamed from the mall, loaded with wrapped packages, colorful shopping bags, and plastic sacks whose mysterious bulges only hinted at the surprises inside.

I should be doing my own shopping, Kate thought. She flexed her fingers inside her frayed brown mittens, hoping to squeeze some warmth into them. Not that I have any money to do that with, she thought. She heaved a heavy sigh.

Books and tuition to jump-start college had drained her meager savings and cut a wide swath in her checking account, and December's rent and utility bills inhaled the rest. The thought of bare cupboards was too much to contemplate, since the ravages of a recent divorce left her finances as fully drained as her emotions. Kate squared her thin shoulders and pulled her coat collar to her chin.

Once classes begin in January, things will look rosier, she said to herself. I'll throw myself into finishing that degree I had to abandon to please Jack, and then I'll get a job to support myself.

She was determined to claw herself out of this pit of despair with no one the wiser. But that meant holding her head high and smiling tomorrow, pretending normalcy as she makes her traditional Christmas Eve rounds to deliver gifts—gifts she hadn't yet purchased and that she had no money to buy.

Now, God, make "cents" out of that if you can! Kate shook her head at the pathetic pun and tried to muffle her bitter laugh.

With closing time near, the throngs of shoppers dwindled along with Kate's philanthropic spirit, which had blown away an hour earlier in the cold Wisconsin wind. A trio of businessmen nodded toward her as they sauntered past. One looked over his shoulder, hesitated at the curb, and turned back. He stuffed a $100 bill into the kettle.

"Pete! Phil!" He shouted to his friends. "It's the holiday season. Show a little charity!"

His friends shrugged and nodded. Kate's eyes widened as she watched them add wads of $50s and $20s from their wallets.

"Thank you," she whispered, clearing her throat to shout "Merry Christmas!" as they walked away.

Kate stared where the corners of several bills poked through the slot in the top of the kettle and leaned over to push them in the rest of the way. Her mitten-covered hand hovered over the cash. This goes to help the poor, she reasoned, and I'm as poor as they come.

Her left hand fingered the crumpled gift list that she had stuffed into her pocket earlier that morning. Her gaze darted to the entrance of the store, then swept the near-empty parking lot. Kate tugged experimentally at the top bill, amazed at how easily it slid free. A $50 bill. She slowly pulled it out of the pot and pushed it deep into her right pocket.

The tip of her tongue darted out to moisten her cracked lips as she tugged at the next bill. It slipped out with as much ease as the first. Another $50.

Kate heard the battered car's windshield wipers snapping in the snow before she saw the actual flakes. *Snow?* She blinked at the fat flakes starting to fall. The car shuddered to a stop right in front of her. With her heart racing and her fingers gone stiff, Kate stuffed the bill back into the pot and watched the others disappear along with it.

An elderly woman emerged from the car and shuffled toward her, her thin nylon headscarf no protection against the wind. The tattered flannel jacket, Kate knew, offered little warmth against the crisp night air.

"Hello, dear," the woman crooned. "What a good thing you're doing out here in the cold."

"Um, well..." Kate's guilty stutters screeched to a halt when the woman pulled a worn leather coin purse from her cavernous handbag. She emptied the purse of its few coins into the palm of her hand and let them clink—one sparse coin at a time—into the belly of the red kettle.

"Merry Christmas," Kate forced herself to say to the woman. "Thanks for your donation."

Her vivid blue eyes locked with Kate's. "God expects us all to see to the needy," she said with a slight shrug and a smile.

Kate watched her car rattle away, tracks trailing in the swirling snow. Like a crystal bell, the poor woman's words rang in Kate's heart: "God expects us all to see to the needy."

She smoothed her toasty coat and tugged her warm woolen cap lower on her forehead. She reconsidered her apartment and the assistance scholarship she had merited. She thought about caring friends and loving family members, willing to help if she set aside her foolish pride and simply ask for help.

Shamed, Kate pulled the hidden bill from the depths of her pocket and poked it back through the slot in the red kettle. She heaved a huge sigh of relief—and gratitude—for her bountiful blessings.

GOD SENDS HIS HOLY ANGELS TO DO FOR US WHAT WE CAN-NOT DO FOR OURSELVES.

A Few Choice Words

My friend Peggy is short and soft-spoken. Her shyness is a neighborhood legend. It took months to get to know her, but it was time well spent. She is wise, witty, and a woman I can count on to take care of my children at a moment's notice—and to take care of my secrets, as well. One day when we were at the grocery store, we heard shouting in the next aisle. Peggy followed me around the corner, and we witnessed the tragedy of a distraught mother screaming at a toddler, and then slapping him in the face.

I stepped back. It was none of my business, after all. But Peggy marched right up to them. She spoke gently to the child, "You're not a bad kid. You are just having a bad day," she said with a warm smile and a pat on his back. Then, she glared at the mother and said in a voice that carried throughout the entire store, "It is not acceptable to hit your child. If you do not stop, I will call the police."

Back in the car, I turned to Peggy and said, "What happened in there? You didn't even yell at the boys who egged your house."

She replied, "Do you know that abused children can grow up to be emotionally healthy adults if even one person acknowledges that the abuse is wrong?" She continued, "I'm afraid to open my mouth in public, but I was more afraid of what will happen to that child if I didn't." I hope that this soft-spoken woman won't be the only angel in that child's life.

Misty

I came home from work to find her curled up on my door-step. Anyone who came by and saw her would've been certain that this was the cat's home. She had decided to keep me before we had ever met.

I was tired, and all I had thought about on the way home was how I wanted to walk in the door, take off my shoes and tie, plop down on the couch, and turn on the TV. I didn't want to think about work. I didn't want to think about anything. And I definitely didn't want to start taking care of some cat.

Misty had different ideas. I unlocked the front door, and she pushed in ahead of me. "Hey! What do you think you're doing?" I cried. She stopped and turned back to look at me as I spoke. "Meow!" was her answer as she found just the right spot on the living-room floor to lie on her back. "Meow!" So I set down my briefcase, kicked off my shoes, and scratched her belly for a minute while I tried to figure out what to do with her.

"Look, you. I don't want a cat! I don't want anybody to take care of! I just want to be left alone." With that I marched to the door, opened it, and invited Misty to take her leave. She came running toward me, and I was sure that my definitive tone of voice had convinced her that she had not chosen her new home wisely. Instead of trotting right out the door, how-ever, she wrapped herself around my legs, purring and rubbing her tail against my pant leg.

When I started to bend down to scoop her up and personally escort her outside, she seemed to know what I intended. Without having a clue as to the floor plan of my house, she ran directly to the kitchen. I followed and found her sitting in front of the fridge, once again making her needs known. "Meow!" she purred again. I suppose she was hungry. I suppose that I was, too. There wasn't much to share, though. I kept long hours at my job and didn't really go to the grocery store very often. I opened the door, and we looked in together. Since I liked milk in my coffee in the morning, there was a quart of milk that hadn't yet soured. I poured a tiny bit into a dish for her and more into a glass for me. We scrounged up a can of tuna from the cupboard, and we shared that as well.

It occurred to me that I was so exhausted, I probably wouldn't have bothered to eat if she hadn't come over.

I sat down on the couch to contemplate the situation. Misty jumped up and sat right on my lap. "What's your name?" I asked her. Silence. She really was a beautiful cat. She was sort of white in color, but not quite. She somehow reminded me of the misty fog that often blanketed the streets when I took my early morning run. "You look like the color of morning mist," I told her. And Misty became my cat.

I'm still not what you might call a "cat person," but Misty and I have an understanding. We're friends. We keep each other company. We eat together. And we take care of each other. I now look forward to coming home from work. And if anyone asked, I'd have to admit that I'm glad that this little furry angel found her way to my doorstep that night.

My Lucky Day

You never know when an angel will appear—disguised as a store clerk, perhaps.

I was just out of law school, nearly broke, and had an interview with a prestigious law firm. I needed a decent suit, so I reluctantly went shopping. I found one I liked, along with a shirt and tie, but I wasn't sure if I had enough money. I went to check out and held my breath as the total was announced. It was exactly what I had in my wallet.

"Very weird," I commented, as I explained the situation to the clerk.

"Maybe you should go get a lottery ticket," the clerk encouraged.

"Not a dime left," I reminded her.

She handed me $1 back and smiled, "I think this is your lucky day."

I've never been interested in playing the lottery, but for some reason I stopped at a gas station and made my purchase. On the way out, I wasn't paying attention and walked straight into the most beautiful woman I'd ever laid eyes on. I apologized, and she smiled. We just stood there, frozen. I could feel that something was happening. Finally, I motioned to the coffee counter and asked her if she would like to have coffee with me. I didn't realize until then that I didn't have any money left.

She ended up paying for the 99¢ coffees. We talked for two hours, and she gave me her phone number. We started dating immediately—I got the job at the law firm and was able to pay for our dates! I knew I'd found my soul mate.

About a year later, we were married. At our reception, we toasted the store clerk—some might call her our angel—who had given me the dollar and proclaimed that it was my lucky day. I hadn't won the state lottery, but thanks to her, I won my personal lottery.

CALL IT A FEELING OR INTUITION. CLAIM IT'S INSPIRATION. BUT THE REAL CREDIT SHOULD GO TO THE INFLUENCE OF AN ANGEL.

Heavenly Father, thank you for the times you've intervened in my life through angels. They are angels, all of them, who bring the reality of your caring heart into the reality of my days. By them, you remind me that you have promised never to leave me nor forsake me. Thank you for the comfort you give through the angels you send.

The Bouquet

I love flowers. My husband, Chad, always brought me daisies—whether it was my birthday, our anniversary, or no occasion at all. I loved coming downstairs in the morning and seeing a vase of flowers.

Chad died three years ago, and no one brings me flowers anymore. I still miss him terribly and know I always will, but I am all right. I have found ways to be happy again.

Milestone dates are still the most difficult, though, and a few weeks ago it was our wedding anniversary. Chad always used to get me a lovely bouquet on our anniversary.

I'd just come home from work that day when the doorbell rang. I opened the door to see a delivery driver holding a floral arrangement of daisies and looking puzzled. "Where's 2302 Bloomington Drive?" he asked.

"There is no 2302 on Bloomington," I replied. For some reason, when they numbered the houses on my street, they had gone from 2300 to 2304. No one knew why.

The driver explained that an envelope with cash and a note had been slipped under the door of the florist's shop the night before. The instructions in the envelope said to deliver a bouquet of daisies to 2302 Bloomington Drive.

He thought for a moment, then handed me the flowers. "They're already paid for. Enjoy!" And with a smile, the delivery driver left me holding a lovely arrangement of daisies. I opened the card. There was no name signed, just a message: "I'll always love you." Although it didn't make perfect sense, it was our anniversary, and Chad, always my angel, had sent me flowers.

Dear Heavenly Father,

Thank you for all the miracles

that I have witnessed this day—

the sunrise and the sunset,

the ability to see this beauty around me.

Thank you for the strength of this body

which serves me so well.

Thank you for the kindness

in this world,

and thank you for the laughter.

Yes, this has been a good day—

I know your angels have been busy,

and I wanted you to know

that I notice how amazing life is.

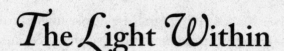

The Light Within

*M*imi had a good job, a nice apartment, and a great car. She didn't have a lot of friends, but sometimes she'd go out for a drink with someone from work. Mimi's parents and her brother and sisters lived six hours away, and she visited once a year at Christmas. They tried to get her to come for Thanksgiving every year, but she told them that it was too long a drive to come for two holidays so close together.

At Christmas, she always arrived with an armload of gifts for everyone, and things went fairly smoothly as long as she didn't stay too long. She could only avoid the questions for so long. "Have you met anyone?" "What do you do besides work?" "Do you want to have a family of your own one day?" Mimi wasn't overly fond of those questions—she didn't even want to think about those things.

Mimi worked long hours. She didn't like television and didn't have any do-it-yourself projects to occupy her time because she'd hired a professional decorator to come in and make over her apartment. She read the paper and an occasional novel, but she wasn't one for spending a whole evening reading. Sometimes she'd rent a DVD. She rarely went to the movies because she didn't like to go alone, and it was too much trouble to find someone who was free and wanted to see the same movie.

So, she was content, she told herself. But she wasn't sure if even she believed that. And that's why the flyer caught her eye. She was running out to grab a quick sandwich from the deli across the street from her office. Normally, Mimi's assistant went out and bought her lunch for her so she didn't have to bother. But today, one of her assistant's children was home sick from school, and she called and asked if she could take part of the day off. Mimi told her to take the whole day. She wasn't sure why she said that, but here she was trying to cross the slushy street in the bitter cold wind. She knew that if she didn't eat, she couldn't work as efficiently as she liked. And work was, after all, the all-encompassing goal in her life.

So that's how she ended up waiting in line at Ralph's Deli that Tuesday afternoon. It seemed like everyone in the surrounding offices had decided they wanted a sandwich, too. While Mimi was waiting in line, she started to read the bulletin board at Ralph's. She saw the usual announcements—lost dogs, lost souls, housecleaners, pet-sitters, portrait photographers. Then, something caught her eye. It was a pale blue flyer for an art class at the local Community Education Center. Mimi passed the Center every day. It was only two miles from her house, so she decided to give the class a try.

The following Tuesday was the first day of the painting class. Mimi wasn't sure why she had come—she didn't know the first thing about painting! She just thought that maybe it was time to do *something*. She was a bit early, as usual, and took a seat in the back of the classroom. People straggled in. Some looked remotely interesting, she thought. There was a nice-looking man. Then a blind woman came in with a seeing-eye dog. The other students greeted her warmly. The nice-looking man got up, offered her his arm, and led her to a seat in the back next to Mimi. "Hello," Mimi said to the woman, "beautiful dog."

"Thank you," she replied, "His name is Baxter."

The teacher walked in, interrupting them. Easels were set up, paints were opened, and everyone was told to paint something. "What do I paint?" Mimi said aloud. She felt utterly lost.

"Whatever you see," answered her new friend with the dog.

"I don't really see anything," Mimi whined.

She quickly became embarrassed, remembering whom she was speaking to. "Oh, I'm so sorry I said that. I just wasn't thinking..."

The blind woman laughed. "That's okay. You don't paint what you see out in the world. You have to turn on the light within your soul and paint whatever your heart sees," she explained.

"Huh?" Mimi didn't do much painting that first night, but the blind lady did. She painted beautiful colors that made Mimi feel something that she couldn't quite identify.

Mimi went back to the class, always sitting next to the blind lady and her dog. Each week, she was surprised by what the blind woman "saw." Slowly, Mimi started picking up the brush. At first her paintings were dark and forbidding. But each week they grew lighter and brighter. The blind lady would ask Mimi to describe them. "Keep looking for your light within," she would say. "You haven't turned on your light yet."

One night, her friend didn't show up. Just as class was starting, the nice gentleman walked in very slowly and explained to the class that their classmate had passed away. She had a compromised immune system and had caught a virus that quickly developed into pneumonia.

Mimi felt a deep sadness within her. She wasn't used to feeling so much emotion. The man walked over to her, carrying the painting that the blind lady had done on the first night of class.

"I was with her before she died, and she asked me to give this to you."

The painting filled her with a feeling of love and well-being. Mimi turned over the paper, and there were words scrawled on the other side:

Don't be afraid of the light within.

Mimi started to cry. The nice-looking man offered her his handkerchief. "Would you like to get some coffee after class?" he asked.

"I'd like that, thank you." Mimi looked at the painting, then at the kindness in the man's eyes. And in that instant, she knew that her light was finally shining.

The Little Angel

I thought that the move to Lakeland Retirement Community would be just the thing for my wife and me. We weren't "old," but we were newly retired and didn't want to take care of a house anymore. Lakeland was a community of condominiums where all the yard work and such was done for us. There were things going on all the time—clubs, concerts, dances, etcetera. And if anything ever happened where we couldn't drive—or didn't want to drive—there were private buses to take us where we needed to go. We also liked knowing that if we *did* need more help, we could stay within the community and move to an assisted living or nursing-home apartment.

I loved to go out walking every morning. There were lots of folks I'd see along the way, and every morning I saw the same people. But we soon noticed that—other than the people out for their morning walks—there was no one outside. There was no need to go out and mow the grass or pluck weeds or plant a flower or two, and so people kept to themselves. And there were no young people allowed to live there, so there were no children anywhere, except for the occasional visiting grandchild.

In spite of this, Lakeland seemed perfect at first. It was everything we had wanted. We were participating in activities and attending dances. There was always someone playing bridge or going to dinner or to a movie, and we met a lot of new people.

Yet, we both felt uneasy somehow. We felt dissatisfied. But we couldn't figure out what was wrong. It was a wonderful community after all, and we had paid a lot of money to be a part of it.

One lovely Sunday afternoon, we were growing restless with the routine and monotony of the community, so we decided to go for a walk on the outside—outside the walls of our gated, secure community. Everything was very quiet in our community, which is a nice way of saying not a single person was outside. We had discovered that the people who walked for exercise did so in the early morning or early evening. Any other time, the yards and sidewalks were empty. It was a bit spooky.

When we walked outside our gates, it was like we were in another world. There were people out and about. Kids were playing, dogs were barking. Without realizing it, we both relaxed and began to breath easier. We walked for a long time. A baseball rolled in front of us and into the street. A little boy started to follow it. Instinctively, I bent down and stopped him. "Let's wait for your mommy or daddy, okay?"

He looked up at me and smiled the biggest, brightest smile he had. An out-of-breath father wasn't far behind.

"Thank you so much, he might've run into the street." He scooped the boy into his arms, and they collected the runaway ball together.

My wife and I continued along the sidewalk in silence for a few minutes. Then we stopped and looked at each other. "Are you thinking what I'm thinking?" I asked her.

"If you're thinking that we've got to get the heck out of that new house and move back to a world where there are children outside, then yes!"

We hugged and kissed and headed home to start making arrangements. Sometimes, it's the littlest angels who toddle into our lives and make the biggest impact.

CHILDREN'S LAUGHTER IS THE ANGEL'S SONG.

Lord, help me keep my heart open to the messengers of your love that you send my way. Through them, you minister to my needs— physical, emotional, mental, spiritual. Remind me that each one is an angel, a gift from your heart, intended to uplift and support me along my way.

THERE ISN'T A VALLEY LOW ENOUGH THAT AN ANGEL CAN'T CARRY YOU THROUGH IT.

A Close Call

After several years of teaching school, I grew tired of coming home from PTA meetings by bus, late at night, in the rain and snow. Usually, as I stood waiting at the corner for one of the two buses I had to take, the lights at the corner gas station would go out promptly at 10 P.M., and I'd find myself standing alone in the dark. That spring, I registered for two weeks of driving lessons, then I bought a car. I also enrolled in a graduate program at a university about 30 miles away.

As a brand new driver, I decided to avoid the highways with faster traffic and join the gridlock of cars and buses on the slower city streets.

On the first morning of classes, the traffic lined up bumper-to-bumper at 20 miles per hour. Since I was afraid of speed, I felt secure traveling at this snail's pace. All I had to do was creep along, closely following the car in front of me. I had no idea of the danger in which this would put me.

After miles of blindly playing follow the leader, I felt the traffic slow down. Then it stopped completely. I looked ahead to see what was holding up our progress and saw nothing but a parking lot of cars.

Then I heard the clang of a railroad-crossing gate slamming down, but I couldn't see it. It wasn't in front of me, and I began to feel prickles on the back of my neck. As I turned my head and glanced in the rearview mirror, my heart lurched when I realized the gate had gone down behind me. The train was speeding toward the intersection as the car in front of me quickly scooted across the tracks. I was left trapped between the tracks and the gates, the nose of my Chevy hanging perilously over the railroad bed. I froze.

"Lord, what do I do now? Please help me," I prayed. This wasn't supposed to happen on my first day of driving my brand new car.

Cars honked behind me and voices shouted, "Get out of the car!" Other drivers jumped out of their vehicles and headed toward me.

I fumbled with the door handle, but I couldn't get it open. "Lord...please," I repeated over and over again. "Lord... please." My teeth began to chatter. Then, miraculously, I heard the click of the lock. The door opened, and it felt like something or someone was pulling me from the vehicle.

As I fell out of the car, hands I could actually see and feel pulled me to safety a few feet away, where I watched my car shudder and shake as the train sped by, missing it by inches.

My legs had turned to jelly by the time the other drivers escorted me back to my automobile.

"Are you all right?" one man asked. "Do you think you can drive?" I nodded and gave everyone my profuse thanks. I took a deep breath as I slid behind the wheel again and drove away slowly. I know now that I will never again follow another car over a railroad track without making sure there was plenty of room on the other side.

"Thank You, Lord," I prayed again, "for a lesson learned and for sending your angels to rescue me."

I've never thought much about angels, even though I've often sung about them in my church choir and read about them in the Bible plenty of times. Is it possible that they really exist? And did God use human angels to help him? Now, there is no doubt in my mind. Now, I have heard them, I have felt them, and I have actually seen them at work.

LONG BEFORE YOU CAME TO THIS EARTH, YOU WERE THE SHINING LIGHT IN YOUR GUARDIAN ANGEL'S EYES.

IF YOU BECOME VERY, VERY STILL, YOU CAN HEAR THE ANGELS PRAYING FOR PEACE.

NOT ALL ANGELS ARE IN DISGUISE. LOOK CLOSER. YOU MIGHT RECOGNIZE SOMEONE YOU KNOW.

Have a Heart

"hat kind of party do you want, Keri?" Her mom's weary smile was easy to see through, even for a six-year-old. Especially one who'd spent lots of time in hospital waiting rooms watching other children and their parents come and go. A kid gets good at reading expressions: anxiety, dread, fear, fatigue.

"Well," Keri drawled, "I've been thinking about something different for this birthday."

"Oh?" Camille's attention piqued. After months at Children's Hospital dealing with the hole in Keri's baby sister, Kadin's heart, it was nice to plan a party. "So, what have you come up with, young lady?"

"I've decided that I don't need any presents," she said decisively. When her mother lifted a questioning brow, Keri grinned sheepishly. "Except for Cinderella Barbie, of course."

Camille laughed and nodded, "Of course."

"But, seriously, Mom. I've got enough toys, and I was just thinking..."

"Yes?"

"I was thinking that maybe people could bring money, instead."

"Keri! I'm disappointed in you," scolded Camille.

"Oh, not for me, Mom. For the hospital so they can help other babies like Kadin."

Stunned, Camille caught her breath. "You mean donate it?" Her daughter nodded. "Really, sweetie? You want your guests to bring money instead of gifts?"

"Yes. Then the doctors can fix lots more babies, and everyone will be happy instead of tired and worried."

Camille was cautious and wanted her daughter to be truly happy when her birthday came around. "You're sure that's what you want? Nothing to unwrap at the party?"

Keri hesitated, but bobbed her head in firm agreement.

Smiling, Camille hugged her selfless, angelic daughter, determined that one Cinderella Barbie would be wrapped and ready, anyway.

God, help me recognize the angels in my life, especially those who come in the form of people I meet. Sometimes, I forget to smile at a stranger or exchange a pleasantry with a store clerk, yet they, too, could be my angels. Remind me to keep my eyes and my heart open to the angels that are a part of my daily life, always ready to offer a loving word or a kind gesture.

Making Mercy Out of Leftovers

Adjusting to life in India was a challenge but was also heartwarming in so many ways. My colleagues at the charity I was working for had turned the guest room on the floor above the office into their vision of an elegant home. I had a one-burner gas ring, a sink, and a used refrigerator that wheezed whenever the power was on—which was about half the time. They were proud of my "Western bathroom" because it even had a shower. I did not tell them that ten drops of water per minute is not a functional shower for a woman like me; I learned to take bucket baths.

Preparing Indian food was a mystery my colleagues were not prepared to share with me. Every lunch hour, at least three women rushed up to my room to cook my lunch, and they took turns being head chef. When I visited their homes, I realized that they cooked over open fires beside their one-room houses. My gas ring and sink were state-of-the-art culinary equipment compared to this, and each of my new friends wanted the experience of cooking in my kitchen.

My contract included room and board, so when I needed food—or when my cooking friends needed a particular ingredient—I rang for the guard, Salini. He was weak and withered, but he seemed eager to complete each errand. He delivered milk every morning in a plastic bag, and his knock on my door was my wake-up call. To me, his smiling face was more welcome than any alarm clock. Although I am not a morning person, Salini's smile made me glad to be starting a new day—even though I knew that after I boiled the milk, I would have to attempt the daunting task of the bucket bath.

I worked through the foreign conventions of Indian culture rather easily, but one issue remained puzzling—I could not make any sense of my friends insisting that I could not, under any circumstances, eat leftovers. I explained that I loved leftovers, and that the refrigerator would keep the food safe from spoiling. Sometimes I pleaded about how I really wanted that curry for supper as I watched it being whisked out the door in a plastic container. "We'll make you more," they always said. And they did, coming to my room after work to make a batch of fresh curry.

After six weeks, I had found a best friend in Vasanti. She took me shopping and to festivals on her motorbike. We shared secrets and dreams. As she was my most frequent cook, I hesitated to ask her about the leftovers she routinely snatched off my table and counter. But finally, I felt that our friendship was secure enough to ask the question.

"Vasanti, why won't you let me eat leftovers? Why won't any of the women let me eat leftovers? You know they won't make me sick."

She thought this over, pursed her lips, furrowed her brow, and finally said, "I'll tell you, but it's a secret."

I promised to keep the secret.

"Salini rides his bike ten miles to work, and then ten miles back. He has a big family and many children. Most days he doesn't have lunch. Some days we give him money for lunch, but we are poor and sometimes don't have lunch, either."

So that's why they liked to eat with me, I realized. I hoped that some day Vasanti would understand how much it meant to me to be able to share my food with my new friends.

But Vasanti was not finished. "Now, we give your leftovers to Salini. He eats every day. He eats some of the food, and he takes some home for his family, and they're better now. The children are not so thin."

I felt doubly blessed that my leftovers were making such a difference for a hungry family, but I still did not understand. "The boss must know how hungry he is. Why doesn't he pay Salini more?"

She shook her head. "I'm the bookkeeper. Salini is lucky to get any money. We are all poor, but we are all lucky to have jobs. Most charity money goes to the poorer families."

I thought of the people the charity helped—families living in huts beside the road, under bridges, under plastic tarps in muddy fields. Every day I saw children begging on streets, their thin hands outstretched, clothing dirty and tattered, expressions hopeless. This was a poor village. There was little to share, and the charity I worked with was a rare beacon of hope.

But after Vasanti told me what happened to my leftovers, I planned harder so I could have more left over for Salini's family. As the weeks went by, I noticed his face filling out, his skin looking healthier. One day he told me his oldest son was going to school. For a poor family, this is a major achievement. I gave Salini a small backpack I had brought for day trips and filled it with granola bars and other snacks I had brought from home. I told Salini the treats would make a healthy school lunch for his son. Besides, in the two months since I'd arrived in India, I had not eaten one granola bar.

Some people may think that this made me Salini's angel, but the truth is he was *my* angel, and so were the others I had met in this foreign land. They made my time in India enjoyable. They taught me to be grateful for what I have and showed me how gratifying it was to help others. And they taught me to always have too much food for one woman to eat sitting on the table or bubbling on the stove.

IF YOU WANT TO SEE AN ANGEL, LOOK IN THE MIRROR, SMILE, AND SAY, "HERE I AM, LORD, SEND ME."

AN ANGEL NEVER GIVES UP. AN ANGEL NEVER GIVES IN. AN ANGEL JUST GIVES.

Angels Seen and Unseen

My first car accident happened about ten years ago in rush-hour traffic on Interstate 5 in Seattle, one of the worst traffic corridors in the country. I had just dropped off a friend after taking her and her children to the doctor, and I was headed home to pick up my father to take him to a doctor's appointment. An unusual coincidence of transporting people, I thought to myself as I pulled into the I-5 traffic.

I was in the middle lane and going under the speed limit, but surprisingly, traffic was moving faster than I had anticipated. Good, I thought, I'll be ahead of schedule when I get to the house. I reached for the levers that controlled the car's fan and temperature, wanting to get some warm air on my feet after the weather had turned suddenly cold and rainy in the afternoon. When I turned up the fan, a bunch of fall leaves that had been lying on the floorboard, which my friend's daughter had collected for me as a gift, fluttered up in the air. They surprised me, and my attention was momentarily drawn away from the road. In that moment, the traffic in front of me stopped suddenly. The roads were slick, and I knew that I wouldn't be able to brake in time. I quickly glanced back and tried to get myself in the next lane. In my state of panic, however, I pulled the wheel too sharply, and my car started fishtailing. Gripping the wheel and trying to regain control, I could feel the swinging of my back tires getting wider and too strong for me to hold the wheel steady.

Moments ago, there was traffic all around me. My car had hit the left guardrail and shot over three lanes of traffic to the right, landing perpendicular to the far right lane, my front bumper buried in the guardrail. But somehow, I had not come in contact with another vehicle.

Amazed and a bit dazed from the impact of the crash, I looked to my right to see if any cars were coming toward me. No cars were coming, but I could see a huge semitruck, and the driver making every effort to maintain control and come to a stop before hitting me. The semi's massive grill was only feet from my passenger door when its deadly momentum came to a halt.

I stared at the truck, numb and unable to feel anything. Then, I had the odd realizations that I'd chipped my front tooth, lost the barrette from my hair, and my glasses were bent. But other than that, I was in one piece, and no other cars had been damaged trying to avoid me. From among the drivers nearby, a nurse got out of her car and came to my aid, staying with me until help arrived. Other than being shaken up, I felt all right, so I declined the ambulance ride to the hospital. Slowly, the miracle of my virtually unscathed condition was dawning on me.

I wasn't surprised that the front half of my car was demolished, but I was surprised when the police officer attending to the scene wrote me a ticket. That was, perhaps, the worst of it. In the tow truck on the way home, fighting back tears evoked by my wracked nerves, I thought about the accident and how the events of the day had been accounted for. I hadn't hit anyone else, the semitruck had been able to stop in time, and there was a nurse right there to help me. She was a kindness from God's hand—an angel of sorts—who brought comfort in the midst of my confusion and anxiety. Angels seen and unseen, I decided, had presided over those moments. Even to this day, when I mentally walk through the ordeal, I cannot see how these events could otherwise be accounted for.

I do not know why the accident had to happen, but my losses, however small, were difficult to accept. My car was just a few months from being paid off, an accomplishment in itself. My chipped tooth was especially disappointing, because I had just had my braces removed—braces I had paid for myself. Maybe it was merely a vanity check, or maybe I was supposed to stop scheduling too many things in my life too close together. Maybe it was a trivial event that was necessary in forming the bigger picture of my life. I will never know the reason, but I know that what happened that day left an impression on my heart and mind about the reality of guardian angels in my life—in all of our lives—and the goodness of God, who knows all things and sends the angels to us.

WHEN WE FIND OURSELVES THE AGENT OF GOD'S GOODNESS TO OTHERS IN THE COURSE OF A DAY, WE ARE PARTICIPATING IN THE WORK OF ANGELS.

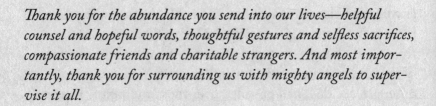

Thank you for the abundance you send into our lives—helpful counsel and hopeful words, thoughtful gestures and selfless sacrifices, compassionate friends and charitable strangers. And most importantly, thank you for surrounding us with mighty angels to supervise it all.

EVERYONE WE MEET IS AN ANGEL IN DISGUISE, EVEN THOSE WHO VEX OUR SPIRITS AND CHALLENGE OUR PATIENCE. THEY, ABOVE ALL, TEACH US HUMANITY AND HUMILITY.

AN ANGEL DOESN'T HAVE TO SPEAK TO BE HEARD, BE VISIBLE TO BE SEEN, OR BE PRESENT TO BE FELT. BELIEVE IN ANGELS, AND THEY WILL ALWAYS BE NEAR.

TO SENSE THE PRESENCE OF AN ANGEL IS LIKE FEELING THE WIND ALL AROUND YOU. YOU CANNOT ACTUALLY SEE THE WIND, BUT YOU NOTICE ITS MOVEMENT, AND YOU KNOW IT IS THERE.

Pass It On

*I*vy was one of the most difficult students I'd ever had to deal with in my second-grade class. She was constantly in motion, tearing up papers, emptying her desk, and removing her clothing. I moved her desk regularly to give the kids who sat near her some relief.

Outdoors, her favorite activities were wrestling with the boys, taking a running leap onto the teacher's back, and running into the far corner of the playground when the bell rang.

In our reading circle, she refused to take her turn to read. Instead, she clung to me, flipped off her shoes and sent them flying, and made loud, disruptive remarks. She needed more help than I could give her, but the special education department had no room for her.

"Why don't you try working with her one-on-one?" the first-grade teacher suggested. With the help of parent volunteers, I was able to do just that. Her reading and math improved, and so did our relationship. She was still a handful, but she was learning, and that was my goal. The following year, Ivy was finally placed in a special-needs program.

Years later I was teaching first grade, and one of my boys, who was obviously very bright, had trouble with his reading.

"Billy, I know you can be a good reader, but you need practice. Ask your mom and dad to help you." Billy merely shrugged, and notes and phone calls brought no response from his parents. One day after school, a young woman stood by the door as the children filed out. She was there picking up Billy, and she stopped me dead in my tracks.

"Ivy, is that you?" I asked the young woman.

She grinned. "I'm Billy's aunt. I want to help him, and my sister could not care less about his schoolwork. But I remember how you helped me, and I want to do the same for him."

As Billy and Ivy left, I smiled to myself. Who could have guessed that the devilish Ivy would one day become an angel to her young nephew?

Read 7/23/21

KEEP YOUR HEART OPEN TO GOODNESS! IT IS POSSIBLE THAT ANGELS PROMPT US FROM TIME TO TIME TO PARTICIPATE IN THE JOY OF DOING GOD'S GOOD WORK.

YOU DON'T HAVE TO PASS AN EXAM TO BE AN ANGEL, BUT YOUR PATIENCE AND YOUR TEMPER WILL BE TESTED WHEN YOU LEAST EXPECT IT.

Reading Davin

Rhonda and her son, Curtis, had grown up together. Giving birth as a teenager and raising him on her own had been tough, but she managed. She gritted her teeth, squared her shoulders, and did whatever it took.

In the early months, that meant sacrificing a social life, which was not always easy for a former social butterfly. But nighttime feedings and studying for a GED left her too exhausted to care most of the time. In later years, doing whatever it took often included working three jobs just to make ends meet.

No matter what, Rhonda treasured memories of the good times she and Curtis shared. In spite of crazy work shifts, college classes, and everlasting financial concerns, they'd always managed quality time together. She counted it as an unexpected blessing that Curtis enjoyed her company as much as she did his. Even through his difficult teen years, she knew she'd done something right.

Now, he was grown and educated, married and settled, and living life apart from her. She knew that it was good and right. Yet, as much as she adored his new wife, Rhonda felt like a limb had been severed. Her sense of loss was profound and she missed him. She missed being a mother—being needed and useful.

Perhaps that was the attraction of her latest job as secretary at the nearby middle school. Rambunctious kids were everywhere, and she loved being surrounded by them. Like a fragrant cup of tea, the students warmed her lonely heart and filled her emptiness. She appreciated their quirky humor, their raging hormones, and even their moody dispositions.

She even appreciated Davin.

Already 15 years old, Davin should have been in high school. Instead, he was stuck in eighth grade, in danger of being suspended for the rest of the school year. He was sent to the office for something nearly every single day. Teachers complained that he was loud, unruly, and disruptive. Students accused him of picking fights, cheating, and even stealing from them.

As habitual as the morning newspaper at her doorstep, Davin was once again sitting across from Rhonda's desk awaiting a verdict and sentence for his latest infraction. He slouched in the red armchair and stared at the hole in the toe of his sneaker.

Then, a classmate walked by and taunted him, "Caught again, Dav?" Davin didn't say anything, tossing his shaggy mane. A teacher walked by and ordered, "Sit up straight, Davin." But Davin pressed his lips together and sank lower in his seat. An aide came by, arched her brow, and chided, "Here again, are you?" Davin narrowed his gaze and glared at her back as he wiped his forehead with the cuff of his jacket, but not before Rhonda noticed the moisture that glistened in his brown eyes.

Davin seemed to shrink into the chair and grow smaller before her eyes. She edged around the corner of her desk, and after a moment of hesitation, she slid into the chair next to his. When Rhonda reached for his hand, Davin jerked back. She simply held on, and as she did, she felt the boy relax and soften. He seemed to melt into her, and they sat like that for a long while.

Davin spoke first. "I'm dumb. Dumb, dumb, dumb."

"Oh, Davin, you're not dumb."

"I am," he said as he shook his head with insistence and swiped at the moisture streaking his cheek. "I can't even read."

"What do you mean, Davin?"

"The words," he explained, "they don't make sense, and I just can't figure out what they mean. Everyone laughs, so I just don't bother anymore."

Rhonda immediately considered the idea that Davin might have a learning disability.

"What do your teachers say about this?" she asked.

"Nothing." His shoulders shuddered with suppressed sobs. "I never told them. I never told anyone before."

How could no one know? It should have been obvious, she thought. This poor kid has been crying for help all along. No longer the bustling school secretary, Rhonda simply did what felt right and natural. She did what a mother does and pulled Davin into her arms and cried along with him.

On that particular morning, Davin didn't face the principal alone—Rhonda saw to that. This time, he had a mentor, a mediator—a mother—to intervene and explain on his behalf.

In no time at all, Davin was assigned to a district reading expert for extensive evaluation. Once his problem was officially diagnosed and the proper teachers were involved, his academic progress astounded everyone at the school.

Everyone, that is, except Rhonda. For the rest of the school year, she kept an eye on this boy of hers, praising him and encouraging him. She was his personal cheerleader, simply doing whatever it took to ensure his success.

In the process, no one was more surprised than Rhonda to discover how much delight they found in each other's company—this once unruly student and the middle-aged school secretary. Quite a reward, she decided, for simply doing whatever it took.

Read 7/23/21

Heavenly Father, just for today, please keep my eyes open, my hands willing, and my heart eager to help everyone in need who crosses my path, even if the need is as small as an encouraging smile, even if the need requires a sacrifice of time and talent. Just for today, God. With your guidance, I have faith that, day by day, I can help more and give more.

Spring Flowers Say It All

My elderly aunt visited me one lovely autumn week. The leaves in my front yard had turned gold, and she said she did not mind me having to work several days during her visit. She loved sipping tea on my enclosed front porch, watching the leaves fall and the birds and squirrels prepare for winter. She did not enjoy daytime television, so I left a stack of Agatha Christie mysteries on my coffee table for her to read, and in the evenings, we discussed the squirrels' antics and the books.

When I hugged her good-bye at the airport, she said, "I'll see you in the spring, and I'm looking forward to your beautiful front yard."

Although I meant to plant spring bulbs that year, I was just too busy. By the time the snow was up to my knees, I received a call from my cousin. My aunt had suddenly died. It turned into a bitter winter, and every time I thought about the spring, I felt a stab of sorrow that my aunt would not be with me to enjoy it.

Around mid-March the snow had melted to leaf-littered patches. One morning, I saw the most surprising thing—there were crocuses in my front yard! I had never planted crocuses, yet the yard soon filled with lilac, yellow, and white blossoms. More and more of them bloomed every day, as if by magic and on schedule.

Eventually, my mailman solved the mystery. He had seen an elderly woman planting bulbs in my front yard the previous fall. She had remarked that I would be too busy, and she had said a prayer that the squirrels would not eat all the flower bulbs. I realized that my aunt was my flower angel—and each spring, her flowers remind me of her caring, generous nature.

———————— ❯❯•◦•❮❮ ————————

ANGELS SPEAK TO US IN THE NOTES OF A HYMN, IN THE SOFT BREEZES OF SUMMER, IN THE VOICE OF A CHILD. WE NEED BUT LISTEN.

———————— ❯❯•◦•❮❮ ————————

TRUE ANGELS WILL NEVER SEEK OUR PRAISE BUT WILL ALWAYS POINT TO THE ONE THEY SERVE, WHOSE LOVE SENDS THEM TO US IN THE FIRST PLACE.

———————— ❯❯•◦•❮❮ ————————

GUARDIAN ANGELS LOVE US, EVEN WHEN WE DON'T LOVE OURSELVES.

The School Angel Visits Sydney

I did not want to teach a special-needs class, but substitute teachers on limited budgets cannot be picky. The call came at 6 A.M. I dressed quickly and casually in the outfit I always have hanging on the back of my closet door for occasions like this. Unlike my honors students, these students would not notice that I was not wearing stockings or earrings. "Paycheck, paycheck, paycheck," I muttered as I parked my car in the faculty lot. The high school teachers had been unusually healthy for the middle of flu season, so it had been a lean month.

The two classroom aides looked at me expectantly. I was the expert, they thought, and I did not disclose that my degree was in literature and my experience in honors English. This morning's lesson was distinguishing between red and green. I asked the aides to teach the students who were easy to work with, and I would teach the most difficult ones. Surprisingly, there was only one they considered difficult, and that was Sydney. He was not physically impaired like most of the children, but his mind was unable to focus on the simplest task. Sydney and I sat in a corner of the room, desks facing each other, and I expected the inattention and angry outbursts of a frustrated child. I sat between him and the door, because some children like Sydney run around the room—sometimes even *out* of the room.

But Sydney sat quietly at his desk. His shirt was clean and pressed, and his posture was perfect. His smile was particularly serene, a rare expression on a child who struggles each day just to dress himself. He seemed to be waiting for something, but what? Not the flash cards with red balloons, cars, and scarves, or the ones with green plants, shirts, and trucks. It was obvious that Sydney did not know red from green, and he would not know by the end of the lesson, the end of the day, or even sometime next year. Yet, his smile did not waver. Unlike me, Sydney appeared confident.

An idea popped into my head. I set aside the flash cards and decided to just talk to Sydney. After each question, he looked at me with great concentration and only answered one question for every ten I asked him. I handed him a sheet of lined paper and a pencil and asked if he would write down his answers. Sydney was able to print simple words. He asked me how to spell "plate" and "sofa." By recess, Sydney had printed a four-sentence story about eating pork chops and rice on the sofa while watching football on TV.

Sydney agreed to read his story to the class. He stood as proudly and confidently as a politician even though not one of his classmates understood much more than the word "TV." Several shouted out "TV! TV!" The aides and I clapped, and when two of the other children realized something important had occurred, they clapped, too.

An aide taped Sydney's story to the board and gave a red marker to one of the students and a green marker to another. James needed a walker to get to the board, and Clarissa had difficulty finding the right end of her marker. They drew large, ragged red and green circles around Sydney's story. One added exclamation points. The other students looked at Sydney, James, and Clarissa, but they were not looking vacantly. Their faces looked as excited as I felt.

Sydney smiled for the last time that day, and he took his seat and sat quietly until lunchtime. The aides and I tried to elicit the slightest response, but his eyes focused on nothing but his story taped prominently on the board.

After the lunch bell rang and the room was empty of students, I asked the aides what had happened. "The school angel came to visit Sydney," one said. The other nodded. "Sydney may not say another word for the rest of the year, but somewhere in his mind will be the memory of the day he wrote a story and read it to the class."

Thanks to Sydney and his angel, I became the school district's special-needs substitute teacher. I anticipate and plan for the inattention and misbehavior that goes with the job, but I also expect the school angel to be on my team of teachers. Only she can help a student experience an hour or two of success in the classroom. Although her visits are seldom, the expectation that she may drop in at any time gets me through the difficult days, and I eagerly wait for her.

"These children need you," the principal said at the end of that first day, "more than the honors students you've taught before." She seemed to be pleading for me to make the decision I had already made.

"I've never seen the school angel at work in honors English," I told her, even though I knew that this statement might make her think I was crazy.

But she just smiled and nodded as if she knew exactly what I was talking about. "Angels go where they are needed," she said. "I hope you will, too."

Good morning, Lord. I have another busy day ahead of me. This may be the only minute I have to talk to you. Please tap me on the shoulder now and then—no matter how busy I am—and remind me that the world does not revolve around me.

THE VERY WORD "ANGEL" MEANS "MESSENGER." IN A TRUE SENSE, THEN, WE OURSELVES ACT AS ANGELS WHEN WE COMMUNICATE THE MESSAGE OF GOD'S UNFAILING LOVE.

Up a Tree

"Call me Old Mother Hubbard, God, because my cupboard is certainly bare," Elizabeth exclaimed, bracing her arms against the porch railing. "Even the toilet-paper spindle is empty."

She raised her face to the grandeur of the starry night sky. "I need a miracle. A miracle, plain and simple. Amen."

Elizabeth was old, but her heart was young and eternally hopeful even in the face of overwhelming odds. She'd found herself in worse situations than this and still managed to keep her faith, even at 82 years old. But until the powers-that-be find her missing social security checks, she was in dire need of food and prescriptions.

"What I really need," she added in postscript to her prayer, "is a money tree." Elizabeth chuckled. "But we both know money doesn't grow on trees, don't we, Lord?"

She shook her head ruefully, shooed the cat inside with her, and turned the lock.

The next morning, Elizabeth rose early to brew her morning tea, re-steeping yesterday's tea bag. Steadying the steaming cup, she headed toward her rocker on the front porch but stopped cold before she reached it.

"What in the Lord's name?" She squinted against the rising sun.

The tall border of ancient lilacs near her house was criss-crossed with streamers of white that looked like giant cob-webs. Stunned, Elizabeth limped closer.

"Well, you did it, Lord! And it's nearly as good as a money tree. Why, you sent some blessed soul to toilet paper my trees!"

And with a speed that belied her arthritic limbs, Elizabeth salvaged the windfall—one toilet paper roll after another—and laughed to herself about the teenagers, her angels, who didn't know they were sent by God to toilet paper her yard.

WHEN WE ARE UNKIND TO EACH OTHER OR TO OURSELVES, THE ANGELS WEEP.

HOW DO YOU MAKE AN ANGEL HAPPY? LAUGH FROM THE VERY DEPTHS OF YOUR SOUL.